Anthracite Roots

Anthracite Roots

Generations of Coal Mining in Schuylkill County, Pennsylvania

Joseph W. Leonard III

THE
History
PRESS

Published by The History Press
Charleston, SC 29403
www.historypress.net

Joseph W. Leonard III
200 Horizon Drive
State College, PA 16801

First published 2005
Second printing 2010

ISBN 978-1-5402-0375-5

Library of Congress Cataloging-in-Publication Data

Leonard, Joseph W.
Anthracite roots : generations of coal mining in Schuylkill County, Pennsylvania / Joseph W.
Leonard III.
p. cm.
ISBN 978-1-59629-050-1 (alk. paper)
1. Coal miners--Pennsylvania--Schuylkill County--History. 2. Anthracite coal industry--
Pennsylvania--Schuylkill County--History. 3. Coal mines and mining--Pennsylvania--Schuylkill
County--History. 4. Leonard, Joseph W. I. Title.
HD8039.M62U6435 2005
331.7'622335'092274817--dc22
2005007558

contents

*This book is dedicated to the memory of our son
Joseph W. Leonard IV,
who died in a mine disaster near
Fairview, West Virginia, on February 6, 1986.*

acknowledgements

To my wife Jo Sunday Leonard for guidance, to my son Dr. Stephen S. Leonard for suggestions, to Leo Ward and The Schuylkill County Historical Society for supplying historic photographs of the Anthracite Mining Industry and to Joy Mining Manufacturing for supplying photographs of bituminous coal mining equipment.

introduction

This book provides an account of a family and community spanning more than 170 years of world coal-mining history. It is an intensely personal story, but can also be seen as the story of all American coal-mining families. It is a story of both success and tragedy involving the local past and the worldwide present. Coal mining is one of the most dangerous and deadly professions; three Leonards were killed mining American coal, including our dear son, Joseph W. Leonard IV.

As a means to limit the scope of my effort, I emphasize family members and their children who were directly involved in the nation's coal industry; less mention is made of my early American non-coal-mining forebears, the Drobil and Jacoby families. My early coal-mining forebears were the Leonard, Bettinger and Brestler families, who emigrated from various states in Germany in the early and middle 1840s. All were members of the working class, Catholic and two patriarchs bore the name Philip: Philip Leonard and Philip Bettinger. Most of my forebears worked in agriculture as foresters, farmers or gardeners prior to their immigration to the United States. Today's descendants of these early families are dispersed all over this great nation and their numbers are too great to be accounted for without the benefit of exhaustive genealogical research. In addition to the Leonard, Bettinger and Brestler families portrayed in this book, descendants of these early coal-mining families can be found bearing names like Jackson, Vining, Carey, Whelski, Sherry, Rummel, Wagner, Daws, Seider, Franzen, Shay, Brown, Johnson and Schum, which is really only the beginning of what could be expanded into a very long list. Today's descendants include members of many Christian faiths, as well as a very broad range of nationalities, including German, Swedish, Scottish, Irish, English, Czechoslovakian, Slovakian, Polish, Italian and Croatian, among others.

In this history the spelling of names is approximately as it appeared in the records and no attempt was made to standardize the spelling, i.e., Leonard and Lenhard, Brestler and Bressler and Beddinger and Bettinger.

By sharing the experiences, triumphs and tragedies of my own family, in this book I provide a personal look at what life was like in the early coal-mining industry and how that industry has evolved and improved to become one of America's most important industries. With the exception of today's modern high-tech bituminous coal miner, I believe that the Pennsylvania anthracite contract coal miner may be the very best of all of history's miners, regardless of whether he mined hard rock, like gold, iron and zinc or soft rock, like coal. The anthracite coal miner mined thick and thin as well as flat, sloping and vertical deposits while using a diverse mixture of the widely differing hard rock and soft rock mining systems. It was not unusual to find all of these complex conditions in a single anthracite coal mine. In addition, he was frequently surrounded by dangerous rock pressures, with the potential for sudden high-risk structural failure. Structural failure could also be caused by the large bodies of water in surrounding mined-out workings leading to a mine wall collapse and deadly inundation. Then there were the ever-present and equally hazardous large bodies of asphyxiating and explosive gas. I submit that this environment describes a level of mining complexity that has few comparisons. The anthracite contract coal miner was at once a weight lifter, since much strength and endurance were required to lift and drag the heavy supplies and equipment hundreds of feet up and down the frequently steep and narrow workings; a carpenter, since the timbers, and pre-cut planks used to build chutes and gates had to be carefully fitted to provide secure constriction to control rock falls; a geologist, since accurate estimates of present and future stratigraphic conditions were important to his economic and personal survival; an explosives technician, since correct drill-hole depth, direction, powder placement and powder weighting within each hole was critical for managing the breakage of coal and rock; an equipment technician, to keep his equipment well maintained; a security specialist, since he had to know the location and use of complex rescue equipment together with the changing exit routes from his current deep, remote and constantly changing location within the mining complex; an emergency medical specialist, since he could

The town where Necho Allen discovered anthracite coal. It no longer exists. *Schuylkill County Historical Society.*

be called upon to administer to an injured or crippled buddy at any time; a chemist, since he had to understand the behavior and management of dangerous explosive and asphyxiating mine gasses; an inspector, to practice safety; and last but not least, a soldier. European nations long recognized the soldiering role of miners, and provided uniforms much like we provide uniforms for our police, firemen and soldiers.

Again, with the exception of today's high-tech coal miner, these are just some of the reasons why the anthracite contract miner must be ranked at the very top of this ancient, difficult and demanding trade.

heroes

1

Brave actions associated with winning causes are almost always the ingredients needed for the making of national heroes—frequently politicians or high-ranking military officers. Winston Churchill is a notable example of an enshrined political hero. Generals MacArthur and Montgomery are examples of respected military heroes. Frequently the most visible heroes, these men are also the greatest beneficiaries. They frequently die of old age after their highly visible exploits, largely performed out of harm's way and are securely enshrined in scholarly memoirs. Next in the hierarchy of heroes, and much less frequent, are little guys involved in winning causes, like Chuck Yeager or Audie Murphy. These heroes lived long enough to attain visibility, after repeatedly and willingly placing their own lives at risk in brave, obscure and noble actions at a much earlier time. Finally, the more typical hero is unsung and may have been drafted or enlisted and sent into battle only to die in some isolated, no-retreat encounter. Only families and friends, on both the winning and losing sides, remember these heroes. But memories fade.

This book is about another kind of hero: the heroes who faced death each day in our energy industry as it positioned itself to launch the American Industrial Revolution, the greatest

Miners at the Eagle Hill Mine, near St. Clair. The year was 1886. Note the hats and the whale-oil lamps. The only purpose this headgear served was to keep dirt and water off of the heads of miners. The open flame ignited many explosions and killed many early coal miners. Use of this lamp killed great-grandfather Philip, who died in a methane ignition. Besides keeping the head clean and dry, it could also warn of carbon monoxide gas. If it went out, miners started running. *Schuylkill County Historical Society.*

of all the industrial revolutions. With great geographic location and rich earth, the United States energy industry is clearly the underwriter of our current place in history. Few heroes compare with those of the coal industry. At best, these heroes faced years of gradual loss of quality of life and health resulting from workplace darkness, isolation, dust and smoke, and the always sudden and ear-shattering noise of the explosions and machinery used to dislodge coal. Sudden or slow death and severe and crippling injury were always present. It was usually present around the mine, and permanently present in the local communities.

The daily concerns of the coal miner were many. Picture yourself as a coal miner, and imagine some of the thoughts you might have. Would miners in some section of the mine fail to detect and remove gas resulting in a chain-reaction explosion that would cause the entire mine to blow up, including your section? Would you be the one to unwittingly cause the explosion? You know that the odds of surviving such an explosion are minuscule. You know that the government passed laws and wrote a library full of reports to ensure that your mine is provided with needed safety training and equipment. But you also know that for you these laws are largely cosmetic and too often merely serve to make people feel good. Can you imagine what it must have been like being a miner through much of the 1800s and early 1900s, long before the government even considered safety? Your many fears were not even addressed. You placed your welfare in the hands of God and prayed. Miners still do that today.

Would undetected weaknesses in the rock and the rock-support construction above or around your workplace cause sudden uncontrolled rock movement leading to injury or death to you and your buddies? Did you use valuable production time to shore-up the rock around your workplace in what you believe to be the safest manner? Are you certain that there is no asphyxiating gas in your workplace? Could you be mining toward undetected old workings with the constant threat of death by sudden water or gas bursts? You know that if you are unable to work your family will suffer. What will happen to the children?

The constant burden of fear is slowly replaced with resignation and eventually with fatalism. You know that fatalism is the enemy of safety, but at least your worry has been replaced by the less exhausting but more dangerous occasional concern. You join with other miners and arrive at work well ahead of the shift change, because you worried about your workplace and did not sleep well, and because this was one way that you could get some badly needed comradeship before the shift begins with its blackness, noise and isolation. You know that for the next eight to ten hours you will not be able to smoke and ease tension; you note that some men join the group and light one cigarette off another. You hear older miners complain about gradually losing their "wind." They blame the powder smoke, bad air and dust. You know that all of these factors contribute to the dreaded life-ending conditions that everyone knows as miner's asthma, and that these words are frequently prominent in obituaries. Some miners recommend washing the dust down with alcohol and claim that their doctor recommends it. You know that some miners are physically limited and are both short of breath and drink too much. You know that they are on their way to becoming the most unsung of the unsung heroes.

Why would anyone work in this early industry? The answer is that early mining was frequently the only advertised opportunity available to families getting off the ships from Europe. The jobs frequently offered free or low-cost housing for you and your family. It looked like a quick fix. After being long unwanted in Europe, here at last was a place where you were wanted, for whatever the reasons. Call it opportunity. You either mined the coal or you sold things to the miners or to the industry. Selling was frequently the best deal—making or distributing all forms of alcohol, tobacco, lawyering, politics and merchandising. The early sellers might succeed or fail but they were generally free to practice their trade in a much less hostile environment.

Perhaps the only difference between the well-known military hero and the unknown coal-mining hero is time. The military hero becomes fatalistic at a more rapid rate. Because of the nature of the danger, it usually takes more time and attrition for the coal miner to lapse into fatalism. The military hero may be given a medal, while the coal-mining hero frequently is viewed in reports as someone whose inattention to the details of his job caused the accident or disaster to happen.

generations of mining in
schuylkill county

2

It was the early 1930s and things were not going well. We were in the Great Depression, and many of the men in my neighborhood were out of work. Pottsville, Pennsylvania, where I was born, was an aging industrial-mining town. It was a small hub city surrounded by a myriad of deep anthracite coal mines and tens of thousands of coal miners and their families. Pottsville was connected to these mines and their satellite towns by a complex web of railroads, trolley lines, first-, second- and third-class roads, trails, foot paths and a long-abandoned but still visible canal system.

In Schuylkill County most roads led to Pottsville, the county seat, and people found it convenient to come there for many of their commercial and professional needs. The Great Depression took a painful toll on the area, as the mainstay Reading Railroad Shops were nearly idle, and only those surrounding mines that could operate at the lowest cost and produce the finest fuel were allowed to supply whatever demand might be left for anthracite coal. It was easier to be cold in the winter than spend precious dollars for fuel. In desperation, unemployed coal miners would illegally extract and sell coal from available and out-of-sight outcrops, wherever they could be found. Such black-market mines were known as bootleg holes and few seemed to care that the coal was not legally obtained. The company police who were still employed frequently looked

A typical early mine entrance at the Eagle Colliery at St. Clair. *Schuylkill County Historical Society.*

the other way. Families spent afternoons picking any lumps of coal they could find off of the many steep and abandoned mine waste piles. Many days of picking might provide a month or two of fuel supply for the winter.

Dad taught me that the good coal was brighter and not as heavy as the waste. With this knowledge and a burlap bag, I became a worthy coal picker. Being a normal boy, I thoroughly enjoyed climbing up and down the steep coal banks, dragging my coal bag, and getting very, very dirty. Needless to say, my patient mother never fully adapted to cleaning up the mess. However, for a few extra bags of coal and daylong relief from boy-sitting, it was probably a good deal for both mother and grandmother.

Not only did we pick coal, we also picked all of the many variations of wild berries that could be found in the mountains, as well as any crops from farms' fields that were open to the public for commercial harvesting. My mother and her mother, Nanna, spent much time in the kitchen preserving our largely scavenged harvest, ranging from blueberries to corn, all of which resulted in many shelves of preserved food stored in our basement. Couple this with a bin full of recently handpicked waste-bank coal at the other end of our basement and we were ready for the winter. We viewed this hoard of supplies gathered at the end of each summer with great pride and satisfaction. This cache would help us toward another year of freedom from a government takeover of our home, and provide our family with another chance to save a small amount of money for a "rainy day."

Both Pottsville and Schuylkill County were highly diverse ethnically, with an incredible mix of closely spaced nationalities, languages and churches packed into a relatively small, hilly area. This sprawling yet highly concentrated patchwork society of separated villages, diverse ethnic people and many hills must have had few equals in the nation. It was at once densely populated, yet with a significant degree of separation. To understand this uniqueness, it is only necessary to understand anthracite geology. Coal veins in places like Pottsville were heavily folded and steeply pitching deep into the earth, reaching depths in places of more than six thousand feet. This folding meant that under each parcel of land there was an almost endless supply of coal. Hence, when more coal was needed, it was simply a matter of mining deeper. This permitted the development of an unusually high population density with a culture of permanence, unlike the more numerous bituminous coal-mining towns, where flat seams forced coal mining to progress farther and farther into rural areas and away from the populated towns.

Hence, anthracite coal geology tended to build enduring and densely packed cities while bituminous coal geology tended to build small villages where growth was more scattered and advanced at a much slower pace, if at all. In the Anthracite Region you could find the Pennsylvania Dutch (Pennsylvania Germans), plus Irish, Welch, Italian, Tyrolean, Polish, Croatian, Lithuanian, Slovakian, Slovenian, Hungarian, Austrian, White Russian, Greek, Ukrainian, Serbian and almost any other European nationally that one can think of. With them came their churches, cultures and languages. Even today, the aging church structures in the Pottsville area offer a concentrated variety that has few equals.

I was born in 1930 on top of a cliff in a long, narrow frame home at the end of a row in a working-class neighborhood in Pottsville. The home was owned by Laura Jacoby Bettinger, my long-widowed maternal grandmother, known affectionately as Nanna. Her husband, Phil Bettinger, was a mine boss at the large Phoenix Park Mine near Minersville, Pennsylvania when he died in 1914 at age thirty-six of typhoid fever. After having earlier lost her daughter Helen at age two, only my mother Gertrude remained of her little family. With her husband's and daughter's deaths, my grandmother's promising start in life ended all too soon. This experience undercut her ability to be hopeful, but it never affected her ability to be patient, warm and loving. Lucky for me, I was the recipient of these wonderful gifts.

An anthracite hand-fired hot-air furnace attended to by my dad, Joe Leonard II, heated all three stories of our home. The regulation of the furnace, especially during cold weather, was under constant review and discussion by both mother and grandmother. If it was too cold or too hot, dad would be the first to know. Hence, one of dad's many domestic duties was to make sure that the temperature was maintained at the highest possible level. This required a skillful blend of mixing coal, fire and air coupled with the timely removal of ashes. It seemed that only dad was qualified to perform this function.

To get home from most of the places where I needed to be (such as school, church, the YMCA, doctor and dentist), it was necessary to walk up a cliff along a one-hundred-step iron stairway and continue to climb the steep street located between the stairway and my home. Four to eight trips a day along this obstacle course were typical. Being a cliff dweller in a home at the end of a row and facing westward had its advantages. Immediately out of our western window I could see the manicured home and garden of a wealthy factory owner; at a much greater distance, there was the stately Pottsville High School located along the horizon. On many evenings this beautiful setting was cloaked in a sunset. The sunsets were especially magnificent in autumn.

Out of our back door, across a valley and glued to Sharp Mountain, I could see the towering Saint John the Baptist Church. Its tower contained five bells of varying size which, when rung on special occasions, sent shockwaves down the spine. The bells were long ago shipped from Germany and required five men to pull the ropes. Each bell was named after a saint. Saint John's was our family's parish and school since 1842. The structure that I could see on Sharp Mountain was built in 1872. What an inspirational setting! Sharp Mountain was honeycombed by more than one hundred years of deep anthracite coal mining. This environment together with our dominant hill-top setting, European ethnicity, commercial, industrial and professional surroundings would challenge the imagination of any normal boy. Much later in life it occurred to me that even the very wealthy could not buy so much cultural, social and natural variety in a single location.

My earliest memories take me back to a time when I was about four, when Nanna would scoop me up on her lap, hug me and tell me bedtime stories. I thought then, as I do now, that Nanna was just about as good as any grandmother could possibly be. Nanna told me such usually reliable stories as *Peter Rabbit, Jack and the Beanstalk* and the *Three Little Pigs*, but eventually, even these stories needed encores. The encores were stories about her life. They were classics that never grew old. For better or for worse, they were to provide me with a future direction for the rest of my life.

The stories that I could never hear too often were those of Nanna's early married life in the small mining village of Phoenix Park. Phoenix Park was one of those many "patches" from which walking trails, dirt roads or trolley rides were required to reach churches and stores in places like Pottsville or Minersville. For a city girl this must have been an adventure. Nanna told me that she and Phil lived on bosses' row on top of the hill overlooking the

Picture of a door boy. He opened and closed doors to maintain mine ventilation and let miners and coal cars enter and exit the mine. This was a boy's first entrance into a coal mine, leading up to the rank of contract miner. *Schuylkill County Historical Society*

This photo shows a deep mine's workings. The very heavy and labor-intensive mine-support construction added much to the cost of mining anthracite coal. Fortunately, the coal was easily the most clean-burning fuel of its time. Anthracite is only surpassed by gas as a clean-burning fuel. *Schuylkill County Historical Society.*

village and the Phoenix Park No.3 Mine. She was proud of her large garden. As in all such remote mining villages of those times, the company owned all the homes, and her lovely home was no exception. After all, what miner and his family would take out a mortgage on a home in such a remote area?

Nanna told me that, as a child, Phil Bettinger went to work as a breaker boy. His job was to discard large pieces of rock from the uncleaned coal coming from the mine. He was pressed into work at such an early age in order to help support the growing family of his father and stepmother. He soon worked his way into the better-paying but more hazardous job of door boy. He would now leave the surface and work underground. Door boys opened and closed the large doors that were installed as air-locks to control mine ventilation. Such doors were opened only when the electric or mule-powered mine trains, supply wagons and miners were entering or exiting the mine.

Ventilation was needed to supply men with air, and to prevent buildup of the dangerous explosive and asphyxiating gasses ever present during the mining of coal. Phil was a tireless worker, and he continued to advance through the ranks from mine loader, laborer, miner, contract miner and fire boss. Both the ranks of miner and fire boss required formal apprenticeships involving lengthy periods of service, after which state certification might be granted. By far the most demanding certification was that of the fire boss, which required extensive and rigorous competitive written examinations. This certification was the doorway into company management. The fire boss had the sometimes-conflicting role of being responsible for both the safety of the miners as well as the productivity of the mine. This put him in the difficult position of being pressured by both labor and management.

Nanna worked in the Pottsville Silk Mill from the time of her graduation from eighth grade at St. John the Baptist Parochial School until her marriage. She told me stories about the sweatshop conditions of millwork. Nanna told me that when the circus came to town the mill owners would coat the windows with opaque

Miners at the York Farm Colliery, Pottsville. This photo was taken in 1891. Although still using whale-oil lamps and soft hats, note the Davy flame safety lamp hanging from the miners' belts. This lamp, invented by Sir Joseph Davies, of Great Britain, saved the lives of tens of thousands of coal miners. It is history's greatest single advance in coal mining. This lamp would permit the detection of all dangerous mine gasses, while giving the miner ample time to take corrective action. *Schuylkill County Historical Society.*

window cleaner, so that the workers would not look out and be distracted. When the circus left town, the owners had the window cleaner removed. All of this rewarded the owners with both more work as well as clean windows.

Members of the Bettinger family probably worked at the Lytle Colliery or an earlier predecessor. In 1948, when I was eighteen years old, Mr. Frank Williams, mine safety superintendent and father of a friend, took us on a visit to this historic mine. With a depth of 2,800 feet from the shaft collar, the Lytle Colliery may have been the all time deepest coal mine in North America. The numerous upper levels were long ago mined out and acted as a conduit for enormous amounts of ground and surface runoff water to enter the mine, making inundation and safety a constant concern. The mine pumps removed more than eighteen tons of unwanted water for each ton of coal produced. With a long history of many deadly gas explosions, and the constant fear of mining under a potential reservoir of water, Mr. Williams must have had many sleepless nights. The Lytle mine was by then more than one hundred years old, very hot, gaseous, wet and extensively timbered. At the time of our visit I had no idea of the historic significance of this mine to both my family and the industry, and how it tied in to Nanna's many laptop stories. The extent to which the limitations of deep coal mining were being pushed forward at this mine was evident even to beginners.

As a boss Phil had to walk many lonely, dark miles underground inspecting each and every working place, frequently beginning at 4:00 a.m., long before the miners arrived. He repeated this routine again during the shift. Only after he found the working places to be safe would he chalk mark the site and allow the miners to enter. He would move his Davy Flame Safety Lamp into selected locations in each of the workings to check for explosive or asphyxiating gas. This life-saving lamp was developed in England by Sir Joseph Davy and consisted of a flame completely enclosed by a finely meshed screen. If gas was present it would leak through the screen. If the gas was explosive it would cause a minor but controlled explosion within the lamp and pop the flame out. The screen would keep the flame separated from the main body of gas and warn of a dangerous gas buildup. If the gas was asphyxiating, the flame would quietly extinguish itself. Either a popping lamp or an extinguished lamp was enough to send the fire boss on a hasty mission to ventilate the area. Frequent detection of gas was bad news. This could mean, among other considerations, that management had failed to take timely action on the construction of costly ventilation facilities or that the current workings were located in a major geologic gas zone.

Phil would also inspect the mine roof, face, ribs, floor and timbering in each workplace. Timber shifted by overnight rock pressure would quickly be noted. Any cracks or loose rock were immediately corrected or red flagged and scheduled for correction at the earliest time. Phil knew that bad things in mining frequently happen out of sight, and that the longer men are absent from their workplaces the more time there is for danger to quietly gain the upper hand.

Idle workplaces could build dangerous gas accumulations and rock pressures, free of immediate detection, to result in tragedy. Phil's job, like those of all fire bosses, carried tremendous responsibility and a great deal of personal risk. After inspection, he would meet the miners as they arrived, frequently at the shaft bottom, and discuss any workplace safety problems that he noted. State mine law required this lengthy pre-shift inspection and instruction session.

Nanna said that during the short days of winter, Phil would go for long periods of time without seeing the light of day, going to work at 4:00 a.m. and returning home at 6:00 p.m. Nanna could see the 1,500-foot-deep Phoenix Park No. 3 Mine shaft head frame from her home, the changing shifts and her husband's walk up and down the hill on his way to and from work. The Phoenix Park No.3 Mine shaft was sunk in Phoenix Park in the early 1860s. The No. 2 shaft was sunk in1839, at a less remote location, between Minersville and Phoenix Park. The first Phoenix Park Mine entry was opened in1831, as an independent mine, driven into rich coal outcrops exposed at the surface.

Nanna had an assortment of favorite foods to pack in Phil's lunch pail to keep him well fed during his long hours underground. A well-embellished lunch pail was a traditional reminder to all observers, and especially to the miner, that he was well loved. In later years, I came to realize that miners' wives were often very good at filling lunch pails, much like a work of art.

Nanna told me that one dark night when Phil was walking home from work along the mine railroad he was confronted by three men, one of whom was carrying a gun. They instructed Phil to falsify mine yardage development to favor certain miners and to yield unauthorized payments. He was told that if he did not do this he would be killed and bad things would happen to his family. Because of the nature of Phil's job, a fatal accident would not be too difficult to arrange. The company police were called in and Nanna's home was placed under police protection. The police told them to keep their window shades fully drawn and be with friends as much as possible. One can only imagine the fear that must have resulted. They knew that determined hit men would have no trouble making good on their threat. The police suspected that the hit men were not local, but that they were imported from some distance, and were part of a secret organization. Phil bought a gun and carried it with him at all times.

To add to this fearsome situation, Phil became ill with typhoid fever and died at the early age of thirty-six, leaving Nanna and my mother Gertrude, age five, to cope with these events for the rest of their lives. In those days there was little government oversight. There were only the incredible survival instincts of very lean and tough people, with some backup support from families, churches and lodges.

My uncles rode the trolley and hiked to Phoenix Park on weekends to help the small, struggling family. They signed Phil's last will and testament. My cousin told me that Phil ended his career as an inside foreman, something he had always wanted. He was buried at Our Lady of Mount Carmel Cemetery at Minersville, Pennsylvania, where his father and mother and grandfather and grandmother are also buried. This very special cemetery contains all of my American Bettinger forebears, an uncommon claim in a changing world. Nanna is buried beside her husband Phil Bettinger III, having remained a widow until her death in 1960. My wife Jo and I attend these graves annually.

There is much that I will never know about the short life of Phil Bettinger. While rummaging through our attic as a boy, I found a mandolin, guitar, banjo, violin and drum. Nanna told me that her husband played these instruments and the piano. He was a member of the four-member Bettinger Brothers Band, a fact that is confirmed by old family photographs. I can only guess that his musical talents were many, but it is difficult to see how he could have continued with this role as his responsibilities at work rose beyond the level of a general coal miner. The great demands made upon his time as mine boss and superintendent made continued activity in the band seem unlikely. Nevertheless, the Bettinger Brothers Band pictures portray a man who appears to be in the mid-thirty's.

As for Phil's early death, other questions remain. Although typhoid fever was not uncommon in the early part of the century, it was less common for healthy people to die from this disease. I can only speculate that Phil may have been weakened through many years of overwork, exhaustion and early neglect, leaving insufficient physical reserves to combat a very serious illness. After all, while only in fourth grade, he was sent to work at the mines to help support the growing family of his coal-miner father and stepmother. The early loss of his natural mother, and being asked to be a man before he was a boy, must have been a heavy burden.

To this day I have one of Phil's mine examination books, the book that he used to prepare for his fire boss examination. The book is loaded with the type of theory taught in my mine safety courses at Penn State. The level of algebra, chemistry and physics presented in preparation for the examination was impressive. With only a fourth-grade education, Phil was undoubtedly very bright, very driven; perhaps he attended appropriate short courses prior to taking the examination.

Although Phil was the most distant of my grandfathers, having died in 1914, sixteen years before I was born, Nanna brought him very close to me. Phil's father had died at age sixty-five from miners' asthma in 1912, preceding his son in death by two years. Phil's grandfather, also a coal miner, died at a very old age. The Bettinger clan is very large and many Bettingers can still be found in the graveyards and telephone directories of Schuylkill County,

Pennsylvania. Family tradition and census records tell a story of a Prussian family that arrived in the United States in the early 1840s. One branch of the family, that of John Bettinger, built and operated the Allar Hotel at the now very small town of Newtown, Pennsylvania. Because there was no Catholic church in the area, they joined a local Christian church until they could build a new church to serve the area's ever-growing Catholic population. This church was known as the Sacred Heart Church and it served the needs of the local population until it was decommissioned in the early 1990s. Father Buehler, its last pastor, was a distant relative and boyhood friend of my father.

The families of the brothers John and Phil Bettinger I were never far apart, and early records show that John's sons lived with their Uncle Phil's family in the Minersville area, while apparently getting started as coal miners in the then-booming anthracite coal industry.

Jobs in mining were plentiful, and any industrious and able-bodied male could have one, provided that he was willing to face a myriad of problems. Layoffs caused by slow coal sales and problems with mine geology cut into work time and income. Hazards were always present, such as severe and permanent injury with the prospect of a lifetime of dependency on family, friends, lodges, charity and church. Then there was the grim prospect of becoming a workforce casualty. To the extent that coal companies were financially solvent, the injured employee was kept on the payroll in some sedentary job such as locker-room attendant, lamp man, records keeper, grounds keeper or company miner.

Economic realities placed a cruel limit on non-producing jobs. Miners who were able to avoid these pitfalls would more than likely eventually lose their health and strength through lung diseases, then known as miners' asthma and now known as black lung, or through accumulated damage caused by years of repeated injuries ranging from hernia to arm, leg and back injuries. The standard industry and medical response to these problems was frequently alcohol, eventually leading to alcoholism. Alcoholics were simply known as drunks and maybe even drunken bums in situations where companies were no longer in existence and where these defeated people were not wanted. Only a limited number of overcrowded poor houses and "lunatic asylums," generally of low quality, were available at the time.

The anthracite mining industry of the 1850s consisted of a few large developed mines and many small independent mines. At that time there was much room for the small mine and the independent coal miner. The independent coal miner could begin his trade with some family support and with only minimal investment consisting of items such as an oil lamp, canvas cap, pick, shovel, hand drills, crow-bars, sledge hammer, blasting squibs, fuse and black powder. With a legal lease, the small miner was ready for business. The small mine, as well as the larger mines, were readily entered from the then-abundant coal outcrops, which were easy to locate along the mountains and valleys.

Mining in the Pottsville Region with its steeply pitching coal veins required much timber, as well as the left-over tree branches, known as laggings, for construction of support systems inside the mine. The laggings were used between the timber to provide additional mine support. Hence, no part of the tree was wasted. Because mine support systems were often the first target of cost-cutting efforts, a high rate of mine injuries and death resulted. Moreover, in the absence of the more costly mechanical or thermal mine ventilation systems present at larger mines, these often desperate and brave independent coal miners had their own way of removing the frequent build up of explosive methane gas: when a suspected gas layer was found near the roof of mine workings, the miner would remove his ever-present canvas cap with its open flame lamp and crawl in under the gas. While lying flat on the floor he would raise the flame into the gas and cause a burn-off. If the gas layer was significant, a mild explosion or even worse could result. Although we know that methane gas is both colorless and odorless, it will always remain a mystery to me how these early coal miners could "see" gas in their workings.

I remember as a boy seeing my grandfather's much younger brother Bill Leonard, with coal-blast dust permanently ingrained into his face. Great-uncle Bill was a lifelong coal miner who remarkably lived to an old age, with his characteristic blue coal-blast tattoos covering his face. These were the unsightly markings, not uncommon among miners in the 1930s, caused by repeated, risky and deliberately ignited methane gas burn-offs. Some of these markings were also caused by flying coal particles resulting from primitive blasting agents and poor blasting practices that were not always well coordinated. With improvements in technology the aging, blue-faced, veteran coal miners, those tough old men, slowly died out and became fewer and fewer as we left the 1940s.

Great-great grandfather Philip Leonard II was born in Germany in 1807 and came to this country with his family around 1844 from Germany, worked as a coal miner, and was killed in a mine explosion in 1851. He is buried in a now paved-over cemetery adjacent to Saint Joseph's Church in Pottsville. Saint Joseph's Church is the second oldest church structure in Schuylkill County, with construction completed by parish members in 1842. The church was and is encased in beautifully hand-carved fieldstone from native rock gathered and sculpted on site by parish members.

Great-grandfather Charles Leonard was born in Baden-Baden, Germany, in 1840, and came to this country at an early age. Charles owned a mine in Patterson, now Brockton, Schuylkill County, from

1868 until his death in 1892. Charles left a family of nine with my grandfather Joe I being the senior son.

Joe Leonard I began mining coal before the age of twelve, when he worked in the family mine, and continued successfully until a few years short of his death at age sixty-two. His mining trade began with family mining, then independent mining and on to the mines of large companies. Dad said that Joe I worked for long periods for the St. Clair Coal Company at St. Clair, Pennsylvania, and spent his final working years contracting for the Sherman Colliery located on Pottsville's Sharp Mountain. Dad said that the best job Joe I ever had was toward the end of his working life as a contract miner at the Sherman Colliery, where he was awarded the contract to recover coal from a succession of prime mining locations. This dangerous job was best performed by a very skilled contract miner with flexible working hours, independent of regularly scheduled mine shifts. When successful, significant profits resulted for both the company and the contractor. Dad said that Joe I was allied with an outstanding team of coal miners as he approached the end of fifty years of work in the anthracite coal-mining industry, and the end of his life.

Joe Leonard I was a contract coal miner, the elite among coal miners. Coal companies employed both company and contract miners. Company miners were frequently older miners involved in mine maintenance such as re-timbering the main and long-life coal and rock tunnels, repairing track and opening ditches to carry away the large volumes of water that forever exited from most mines. Company miners also provided permanent ventilation construction, ran the mine locomotives and undertook general maintenance. Company miners were frequently paid a flat wage.

On the other hand, contract miners frequently did the work that involved drilling, breaking and loading both coal and rock. They generally worked at advancing and developing the mine and recovering the coal. Developing the mine was slow and dogged and involved the driving of many miles of entries, while recovering the coal was much more intense, shorter in duration and highly productive. If it were possible to look through the earth at a developed anthracite coal mine it would bear a strong likeness to the map of a city. In anthracite mining the main streets were known as tunnels if driven in rock, as gangways if driven in coal. Secondary streets that exit at right angles off of the main streets were known as breasts, while tertiary streets that exit at right angles off of the secondary streets were known as monkeys or headers. Hence, the developed openings were equivalent to city streets while the very large remaining solid blocks of coal within the developed openings were equivalent to city squares.

Soft coal mines were laid out in a similar manner with the exception that they were usually flat. Coal transport systems were more uniform, relying on mobile equipment and conveyors, and terminology is different. The large remaining blocks of coal pillars kept the mine from collapsing, while the many "streets" permitted the miner safe passage to and from his workplace as well as a safe haven during the frequent blasting involved in both the development of the mine and recovery of coal. Certain streets also had to share the double function of acting as conduits for the removal of the broken coal product from the mine. Mine cars and long sloping miner-constructed wooden bins transported the coal out of the mine, thus safely dividing men from material. Mine cars were used in the always-flat main streets, while the wooden bins were used in the nearly always upward sloping secondary streets.

The wooden bins were progressively constructed by the contract miners as the mine face was advanced up the slope and into the virgin coal. Coal between the mine face and the mine cars was blasted from the coal face and let fall into the bin where it was initially stored. Miners stood on the broken coal at the top of the bin when working at the face. When these secondary streets reached their limit, the filled coal bins and the yet-to-be-removed coal pillars were now ready for harvesting. It was now time to reap the rewards of the long drudgery of mine development. The bins containing the previously broken coal would be opened and the coal allowed to flow into the mine cars below. Next, the pillars would be blasted and the newly broken coal also moved into the bins for subsequent loading. There are many ways to break the pillars and deliver the broken coal to the chutes. For example, one method is to drill long holes along the length of the top pillar facing the chute, loading the holes with dynamite and blasting off long slabs of coal. These slabs may be several feet or more in thickness. This method of breakage would be repeated to some predetermined point, after which the same cycle would be performed on the next lowest pillar, etc. The new concern for the contract miner was finding enough mine cars to take away the payload. The trips to the bank could be most enjoyable.

Within a relatively small area, the developed anthracite coal mine could be flat, sloped, steeply sloped and even vertical, or a combination of all of these conditions. Flat mining, which was almost always the rule in the much more abundant bituminous coal-mining areas of the world, was almost nonexistent in Schuylkill County, and when found, was usually only a temporary condition. In the few areas that range between flat and mildly pitching, sheet iron was laid along the pitched floor so that coal would slide down the slope to the next loading point. Many areas of the world use sheet iron to transport broken ore down shallow mine slopes. In my travels I observed these methods in places like South Africa and South America. Since many mining areas in Schuylkill County were steeply pitching, miners had to have considerable physical strength to drag timber, flat board, heavy supplies and equipment up the long slopes in order to support mining development.

Contract miners were noted for their powerful physiques, and Joe Leonard I was no exception. When the mine was being developed, contract miners were usually paid a negotiated wage based on the lineal yardage that they were able to mine. However, when recovering the coal they were usually paid a negotiated wage on the basis of the coal tonnage that they were able to produce, either on a raw or clean coal basis. Recovering the coal involved the dangerous, highly productive and sometimes lucrative work of removing the remaining coal pillars from the mine. This operation is known as "robbing."

Mine ambulance, used to transport the injured and dying to the local hospital. *Schuylkill County Historical Society.*

Coal pillars that supported the mine roof were removed according to preplanned and systematic patterns. The pillar-removal practices left increasingly fewer and smaller roof support pillars or stumps, resulting in considerable stratigraphic deflection. This deflection could occur in the roof, pillars or floor or in any combination of the three locations. Such deflections would increase pressure, at times nearly explosive, and the force of gravity would eventually cause the roof to fail. Successful pillaring would cause the roof to fail in a generally predictable manner. Controlled failure called for great mining skill and much personal bravery, since the contractor and his buddies were always working near the "pillar line," removing those pillars.

Controlled mine roof failure is accompanied by a steady, sometimes scary drumbeat of noise caused by the intermittent roof rock falls in the mined-out areas on the other side of the pillar line. Sometimes the breaking up of the roof is massive and the resulting noise, wind and pressure waves can frighten even the most hardened

John L. Lewis, president of the United Mine Workers of America, speaking to visiting college students in Pottsville in 1951. Lewis said his goal was to have the highest-paid coal miners in the world and that he was not interested in protecting jobs. He served as a model for our present labor leaders. *Schuylkill County Historical Society.*

coal miner, resulting in an undignified group foot race to safety by protective passages. If roof failure does not occur as expected, the hanging roof might cause a scary overhang and exert a very high-pressure and dangerous "nut-cracker" effect along the pillar line making mining conditions untenable and subject to serious review. One condition that could cause this bad sequence would be a very strong and rigid roof. If this "hung roof" could not be induced to fail, the section might have to be abandoned with a great loss of coal and frequently serious economic consequences. After all, much investment was expended to reach "pay-dirt," and failure to win this coal represented a loss to all concerned.

Contract miners could work as individuals or they could enlist other miners as part of a contracting company to undertake larger jobs. Joe Leonard I engaged in both types of contracting. The contract miner, working either with a buddy or in a team, would strive to achieve record production while removing as much coal as possible. Productivity and recovery were not only financially rewarding, but by performing well in these areas the contract miner enhanced his chances for obtaining the future cream of any available mining prospects. The best prospects were those locations with a reputation for having workable mine roof rock and "runny" coal. Runny coal flows freely after blasting. These choice locations could result from conditions ranging from favorable geology to depth-related roof rock pressures that assisted the miner in "squeezing" the coal out of the seam with very little mining effort. One contract miner explained this action to me as being somewhat like "squeezing mustard and ketchup out of a hamburger." Such choice locations meant that the contractor might get high coal production with reduced effort, supplies and explosives, to enrich his bottom line.

Much confidence and trust was placed in the contract miner. The contract miner frequently used the always-present neighborhood bar as his office. Mines and contractors tried to keep their best miners employed, even when work might not be immediately available. Miners good at pillar robbing were always in demand. Barroom meetings combining business with pleasure took place after work and before going home for supper. The contractors always bought the beer. Dad told me that Joe I would put a keg of beer and catered food in his front yard for all comers on the Fourth of July and other summer holidays. He sounded like a good neighbor.

Joe I continued to work as a contract miner before the ravages of fifty years of coal mining finally drove him to his sick bed at age sixty and to his death at age sixty-two. According to newspaper articles in the *Pottsville Republican*, Joe I was confined to his home for "some time" prior to his death, because of disabilities brought on by miners' asthma and other job-related injuries. Dad told me that Joe I had not only a severe rupture that required him to go to work wearing a steel belt but also the usual coughing blood and shortness of breath associated with miners' asthma. One morning in 1932, Joe I called my dad upstairs to his room, got out of his bed, hugged him and died in his arms. This at once great, obscure, loving, faithful and at times angry man quietly joined the ranks of our nation's heroes. This was almost always the final story of a coal miner who was successful enough to live through the perils of coal mining and last into his fifties or sixties. I was two years old when my grandad Joe I died, and as with my grandfather Phil Bettinger III, I never had a chance to know these heroes.

Many contract miners, sensing their declining physical health voluntarily retired from this dangerous and unhealthy work when in their forties and early fifties. They would take pay cuts and try to find jobs as company miners or surface employees, or they would completely leave the industry and take whatever jobs they could find. Joe I worked long past the point of no return, possibly in order to make up for depleted retirement resources expended in raising his three-generation family. For these and many other reasons, I am immensely proud to bear his name.

My great uncle John was killed at Kaska-William Colliery near Brockton, Pennsylvania, on August 17, 1896. He was sixteen years old. The accident, investigated by the Pennsylvania Department of Mines, reported that John was killed by "falling under a loaded car." In fact he was killed by a nervous mine mule that unexpectedly lunged forward while John was placing a triangular sprag under a mine car wheel to act as a brake. Placement of the sprag was critical to stop the heavy mine car from rolling out of control, but a mine mule's unexpected behavior is part of the risk. Had the mine management supplied sprags pierced on the side with a length of metal rod, John could have stood at a safe distance from the mine car and positioned the sprag with no risk. The absence of this simple safety device took the lives of many miners, and was an accident waiting to happen. Dealing with the too-frequently badly treated, blind and temperamental mine mules of that time was an inherently hazardous job. According to reports in the *Pottsville Republican*, John was carried out of the mine and taken to his home where he died three hours later of severe injuries.

The Pennsylvania Department of Mines, which was a pioneer in public attempts to make mining safer, preceded the federal United States Bureau of Mines (USBM). The USBM was formed around 1908, as a result of the Monongah Mine disaster at Monongah, West Virginia, which took the lives of more than three hundred men. The slaughter of men mining coal now became a national issue.

Sometime between the mining efforts of Charles Leonard and his son Joe I, mine labor unions began to emerge. When the independent coal miner could no longer find small, easy-to-mine and affordable coal outcrops near his home, either because of local depletion or hostile ownership, he would frequently find work with a larger independent operator. When these operators eventually experienced the same problem, the trend toward larger mines was irreversibly set in motion. For the first time, commitments of large amounts of capital and blocks of coal were needed to provide a stable supply and maintain the large and ever-growing anthracite-based energy infrastructure. The new large mines were often far from home, deep and employed hundreds of men who entered the mine through a few costly, deep and common portals. The financial commitment of the operators was long term and difficult to reverse, while the commitment of the miner was more flexible. For the first time men from vastly different cultures and outlooks were brought together during shift changes and in mine elevators. They were also together on "man trips," riding in coal cars to reach their workplaces and the washhouse. With little in common and freed of the earlier unifying family and cultural relationships of the independent miner, workplace complaints served as a new basis for group discussion and unification. We were entering the golden age of the washhouse orator. These orators were frequently gifted complaint managers, promoters and organizers with a gut talent that may have considerably exceeded those of their nominal managers.

Mine labor walkouts involving disputes over working conditions, safety, jobs and money were now a fact of life and clearly out in the open. This group behavior was on its way to eventually being institutionalized in the form of our first local and eventually our current national mine unions. Mine management frequently countered this trend toward organization by putting their best and brightest washhouse orators on the company payroll as mine managers, where they were now paid a more stable wage to cope with the very unruly problems that they themselves helped to create. Sometimes it worked, and sometimes it didn't. Nevertheless, the time of labor organization and unions had come, the offspring of which continue to the present.

coal mining at home
and abroad

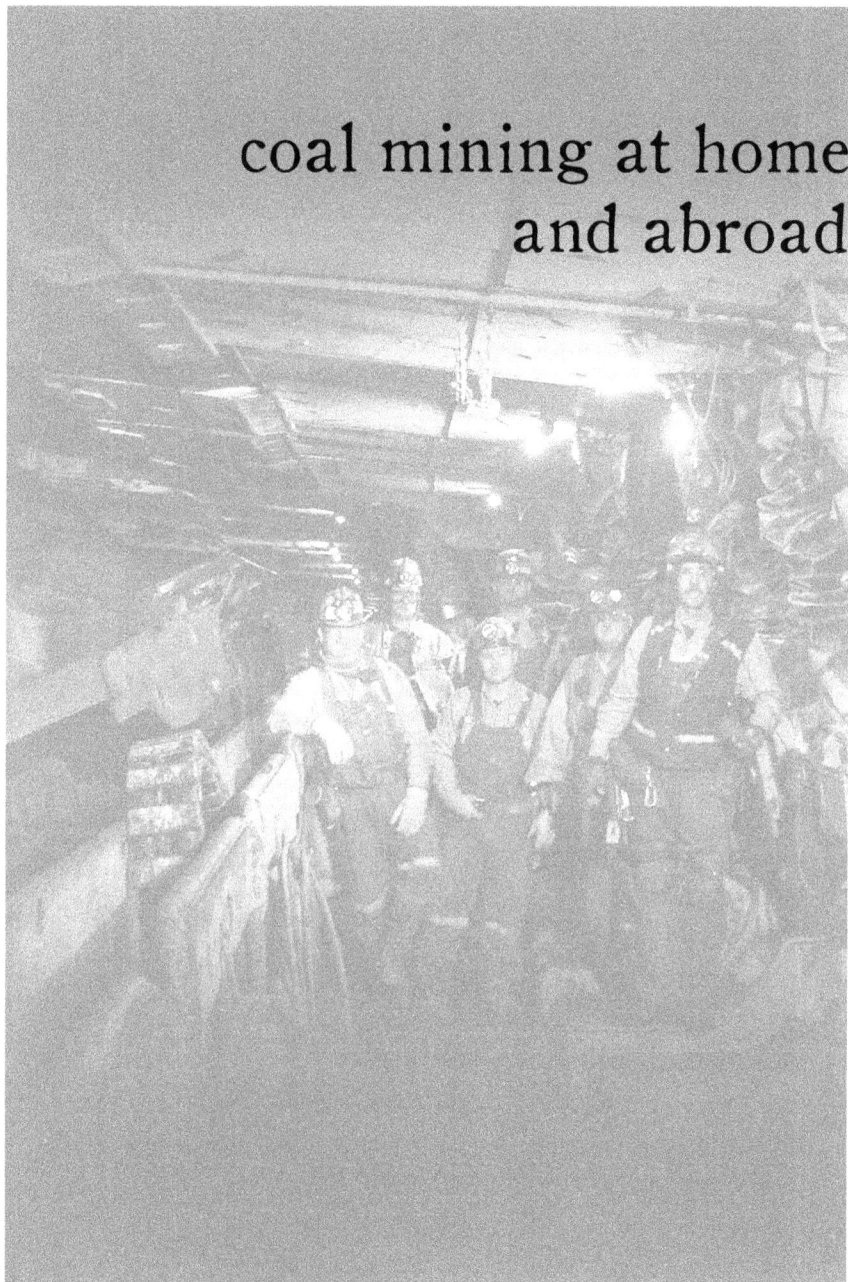

3

I will not forget the second level of Pine Knott Mine, Minersville, Pennsylvania, in the 1950s. While making the rounds with Joe O'Neill, the section boss, we noticed a buildup of troublesome water in the ever-present mine drainage ditches. To find the source of the buildup we rode the electric-powered mine locomotive back toward the shaft. The water kept getting higher. When we reached the shaft we found a torrent of water and debris slamming off the roof of the waiting mine cage, or elevator. Apparently, the water was coming from the first level, which did nothing to help our situation. We knew that the shaft was no longer a viable escape route for the ninety-plus second-level miners working high up in the breasts, and who were not likely to be aware of the pending disaster. The locomotive was no longer dependable, since the ever-rising water would soon short out our power and limited lighting.

The sixty-year-old Joe O'Neill and I took off running, at the fastest possible pace, headed for the most remote reaches of the mine. We knew that the only remaining approved exit from the mine was up an old 1,700-foot slope known as the "Burma Road," which opened at the top of a mountain. Clearly, we were facing a mine inundation of potentially historic proportions. We ran up and down breasts and crosscuts warning the other miners, until we were sure that all of our miners were out. The rising level of very cold water in the main gangways was now flowing in a reverse direction. The water contained much debris, since any wood used to support the gangways began to come loose and float. This unreal situation is like going fishing and suddenly witnessing a long-familiar river reverse its direction of flow.

All of these events added to the increasingly grim and depressing scene. It took more than an hour to clear out all of the men. Everyone helped. Word was passed from one buddy to the next. Men coming out of the "Burma Road" were exhausted from the long climb. Joe and I were among the last out. The lower gangways were completely flooded, and the flooding would continue for days until the entire second level of the mine was totally underwater. I cannot ever remember a time when I ran and climbed so fast, prayed more intensely and prepared for the worst. Clearly, we had to get everybody out. We learned that two first-level miners were killed when the floodwater broke through their workings. It was like being hit directly by a cannon ball.

We were later told that the engineers knew that this area was located beneath a large, long-abandoned and water-filled surface mine. Hence, the engineers made provisions for leaving a large coal pillar and safety zone between the bottom of the water-filled surface mine and the active workings. To make certain that nothing was overlooked, repeated underground diamond drilling around the collapsed section, as a means to test for unmapped bodies of water that might be in close proximity to the actively mined areas, showed nothing out of the ordinary. Old mine maps going back one hundred years failed to show a deeply penetrating slope driven in the late 1800s. This uncharted slope acted as a conduit for emptying the large and hydrostatically powerful body of water from the surface mine into the actively mined workings of the first level. Other than a routine report about two missing coal miners and a "rush of water," this incident received little coverage in the media. I guess it was all too routine, and not good for the image of a vital industry. The inundation filled the entire second level.

It took six months and two giant pumps to remove the water and several months of inside maintenance before the mine would once again be productive.

Many folks never forgot the company paymasters of the early 1950s. Twice a month they arrived at each mine with hundreds of thousands of dollars in cash. They came in three red Chevrolet automobiles with an entourage of company cops carrying Thompson submachine guns, shot guns and pistols. The cops spread out around the mine while the paymaster set up shop in the lamp house. As the miners came off shift they would return their mine lamps, be identified by the lamp-man, pick up their bag of cash and sign the payroll sheet. A few wives with kids, for whatever the reason, would gather near the pay station to make certain that dad made money available for family operation. It was well known that payday was drinking day, and the many barrooms located in the region looked forward to payday at the mines. Drunken, or near drunken coal miners, were often reckless with their money, and not all bartenders were honest. Much family money was lost in mine bars on payday. Paying in cash supplanted the older method of paying in script. Script tied the miner and his family to the company store, which also outlived its usefulness due to corruption. Miners had to be very careful, since their money was in great demand, both legally and illegally.

I made many visits to the deep coal mines of Western Europe in the 1960s and 1970s, and viewing the technical frontiers of coal mining was unforgettable. Visits to the mines of the United Kingdom were special, since this was the land that contained the coal that ignited the Industrial Revolution. This insular island fortress initially bulged with huge quantities of rich, highly visible and easy-to-mine coal deposits located under or around population centers with an almost unlimited supply of labor. Add to this the invention of the steam engine to make power, the Bessemer converter to make steel and the growing demand for both power and steel to supply close-in markets, and the ingredients for the revolution were in place. Only Germany came close as the ideal site for the birthplace of the Industrial Revolution, but Germany initially lacked the steam engine and Bessimer, as well as the protective insularity of the United Kingdom. The United States and the Russian and Ukrainian industrial revolutions were delayed because under-developed transportation infrastructures, which limited the integration of very large but not always ideally located coal deposits.

I arrived in the United Kingdom toward the end of their golden age of coal and at the beginning of their new age of oil and gas resulting from the discovery of oil in the North Sea. The very old and deep mines of the United Kingdom were in difficulty at the end of World War II because of years of depletion of their easily mined reserves, very high costs and the inability of industry to raise the capital needed to renew the industry. To continue to support the energy needs of the nation, the British National Coal Board was formed. Although mine costs continued to be high, resulting in high fuel costs, the mines were renewed and national fuel self-sufficiency was assured. England, like continental Europe, was showing us the future of coal mining and, as in the past, would supply us with both knowledge and equipment.

One unforgettable and characteristic feature about the British coal-mining industry was their mine floors, which frequently consisted of soft clay. The mine at Bilsten-Glenn, outside of Edinburgh, Scotland, was typical. During my visit to this very wet mine, I had the pleasure of being escorted by the lively Jimmy Cowen, an all Britain soccer player. Mine support jacks, which were used to support the roof after the coal was removed, would come under great pressure and slowly sink into the soft-clay floor behind the active mining areas. This resulted in increasingly lowered mining heights as the roof was slowly squeezed toward the floor, making it difficult to enter and exit production areas.

Hence, after only several months of mining, a mine crew could no longer walk upright into their workings, but would have to either walk bent-over or crawl. To offset this slow and certain closure, floor-shoveling crews were used to continuously shovel-up the floor as a means to maintain the mining height along the walkways. It was indeed strange to walk along at the bottom of a long narrow slot, while looking off to the side where the mine conveyor belt was running on the old floor located usually at shoulder height. All of this added to the burden of British mining costs. Today, only twenty mines continue to operate in Britain, under a private corporation, which produces about twenty-three million tons of coal per year.

Visiting mines of Wales was like being back home in the Pennsylvania anthracite industry. Like in Pennsylvania, much of their coal is located in veins slanting deep into the earth. The dialect of the miners bore a similarity to those of our Welch miners in Pennsylvania. No wonder so many of our early mine bosses in the American anthracite industry were imported from Wales. They were the first big-time anthracite coal miners! I remember Gwilliam Williams, and his Minersville, Pennsylvania, contract miners, who took time off from their sweaty work to sing Welsh ballads to any and all visitors to their work section.

Like bituminous coal, anthracite coal formation begins in ancient flat-lying swamps. For anthracite to form, the aging flat-lying bituminous deposit must be under exceptional pressure. This happens when geologic forces fold the flat-lying earth into mountains. That's why anthracite coal is almost always found in steeply folded mountainous areas, like eastern Pennsylvania and Wales.

Bituminous coal may also be found in mountainous areas, but the strata are almost always flat, with little folding. What appears

Photo of the old Pine Knott Cleaning Plant. The author apprenticed in this mine, but the cleaning plant was no longer in existence, having been closed in 1929. This plant was located near Minersville. *Schuylkill County Historical Society*

to the casual observer in bituminous coal-bearing regions as mountains and valleys are neither mountains nor valleys; they are ancient geologic erosion ruts formed by millions of years of water rushing across the original flat-lying surface. The "mountains" are the water-erosion-resistant "stubs" of the ancient flat areas, while the "valleys" are the washed-out troughs, where today's streams and flood plains are located. The open space of these valleys once contained the approximate rock mass formations that now occur on the adjacent hills. The valleys that replaced these long-ago washed-out rock formations now provide a conduit for water and a base to support civilization. Much of this phenomenon can be readily observed when driving on roads cut through hilly coal-bearing regions. The washed-out coal-forming material probably flowed downstream, mixing with sand and clay, where it eventually settled in river basins and deltas to later become gas and oil.

Wales was the first place to mine and transport coal, by rail and ocean-going ships, to the international markets. Cardiff was a major port for early Welsh anthracite coal transshipment. The seaboard areas of the United States and Canada were buying low-cost Welch anthracite in the first half of the 1800s, instead of from the more abundant and much closer American anthracite mines. With no railroads and an undependable canal system, America lacked the infrastructure to connect big markets, like Philadelphia, to the coal fields only one hundred miles away. Today, there is only one large deep mine operating in Wales. Both Welsh and Pennsylvanian anthracite operations are on long-term hold, waiting for the fossil fuel scenario to unfold.

The mines of The Netherlands and Belgium, now no longer operational as a result of huge natural gas discoveries, had problems that were the opposite and even more inhibiting than those of the United Kingdom. They had bad mine roofs that consisted of poorly consolidated sediment overlaying the coal, which tended to quickly degrade and fall into the workings—a very dangerous condition that required elaborate and costly mine roof support systems in every underground opening. Loose strata delayed the sinking of ventilation shafts, because this type of excavation was like trying to dig a hole in water. Such shafts were costly and required special reinforcement to remain open. Ventilation in these mines was pushed to the limit in order to delay the sinking of costly ventilation shafts. The environment in these three-foot-high coal mines was cramped, hot and gaseous. To understand the geology of this area it is only necessary to recall that The Netherlands is a land partly recovered from the sea. It is a land where dikes, pumps and dredges are used to hold back billions of tons of water, sand, mud and silt. It is likely that these same conditions exist in mining districts of The Netherlands and Belgium, but in a much older and more consolidated form.

I will not forget my many visits to the deep mines of Germany, and receiving there an education on environmental management. The Germans are masters at undermining cities in the Ruhr, with little or no damage to surface structures, while recovering 90 percent of their coal. I saw a graphic display of their mining skills on film. As underground mining advances, at depths of three to four thousand feet under an industrial smoke stack, the stack tilts an inch or two in one direction and then an inch or two in the opposite direction, before again becoming vertical. This most convincing demonstration is great therapy for the mining engineer, who doesn't always have full control over his design.

The German mining industry continues to develop an unending supply of highly specialized mining products and equipment. My visits to the European mining industry were frequently as a consultant to examine the feasibility of applying their latest specialized products to specific American mining practices.

I remember visiting an experimental mining section at the Frederich-Wilhelm Mine in Germany, where two flat-lying miners operated an advanced mining system in twenty-four inches of mining height. The system, which was completely automated, shaved thick layers of coal from a prepared block of unmined coal hundreds of feet wide and several thousands of feet long. The ventilation was good and working conditions acceptable, as long as one continued to lie flat and did not attempt significant movement.

Germany was blessed with generally better coal mine geology than that of their more westerly European neighbors. Their mine floors and roofs tend to be stable, and the coal generally of higher quality. Since Germany never has been endowed with significant oil and gas reserves, they continue to support their higher-cost coal industry in order to maintain a certain level of national energy self-sufficiency.

The high cost of deep coal mining in much of the world versus the low cost of coal mining in America is a direct result of poor transportation infrastructure, environmental mandates, depth, age, exhaustion or poor geology. High politically or economic-mandated levels of coal removal can affect strata control and burden mine costs with more equipment and supplies. Stand near a mine and watch how much coal comes out, and how much inventory is sent back in. Modern high-production mines always have large amounts of coal output with relatively small amounts of inventory input. I can think of no other quick evaluation about the condition of a mine than this simple coal output versus inventory input observation.

A surprising fact about western European mining today is that Europe's largest deep coal mine is in Spitzbergen, Norway. Located between the North Pole and the Arctic Circle, production exceeds one million tons of coal a year using American mining equipment.

The modern coal-cleaning plant is an engineering marvel. It will sort and separate billions of particles each day, placing each individual particle in its intended location. A single stream from the mine goes into the plant while two or more streams come out of the plant. One outgoing stream is refuse while one or more of the streams is clean coal product of varying levels of quality. Depending on the investment made in the plant, particle placement can be very efficient ranging as high as 98 percent.

The cleaning plant will break the mine product to liberate the clean coal from the non-coal particles, and separate the liberated particles so that the non-coal particles are discarded. The clean coal particles are then shipped to various markets for final utilization.

Breakage is achieved by a wide assortment of unit operations, some of which may tumble, crush, hammer or employ attritional breakage to achieve the precisely desired result. Separation of the liberated particles is generally based on the density of each particle. Since the non-coal particles are denser than clean coal particles, complex mechanical processes are used to simulate a density between the light clean coal particles and the more dense non-coal particles. Hence, when the liberated particles are fed to these processes the light particles float out of the process while the more dense particles sink where they are dragged from the unit and discarded. These separations are like tossing a mixture of stone and wood into a tank of water: the wood floats while the rock sinks. Usually either violently pulsating water, or suspensions of finely ground magnetite in water, is employed to act as the parting medium to separate the clean coal particles from the non-coal particles. Since the final product from the cleaning plant will be soaking wet, both mechanical and thermal processes are used to achieve the desired level of de-watering. Many other processes are used in coal-cleaning plants, some of which may include chemical cleaning, magnetic separation, agglomeration and dispersion. The coal-cleaning plant is by far the greatest single investment made in coal mining, sometimes costing as much as $100 million or more.

In the deep bituminous coal mines of central Pennsylvania in the 1970s, normal panic limits were exceeded due to a "cutter." The economics of mining in this area frequently called for the simultaneous driving of ten or more parallel entries into outcropping coal seams. Each entry was later joined by crosscuts to form large blocks of coal, or pillars. As the advancing multiple entries penetrated to increasing depths, critical pressures would build up along the outside corners of the roof of the first and last entry. Eventually the roof along these outside corners would begin to fail because the extraction of coal from the multiple entries forced the remaining coal pillars to support the same weight of overburdened rock that was once supported by the unmined coal. Even with favorable roof and floor conditions, this resulted in increased stress on the pillars, causing compression and incremental pillar deflection. For example, a coal seam that was once six feet thick might now contain maximally compressed pillars with a thickness of only five feet, ten inches. This two-inch vertical deflection caused severe cutting stresses along one or both of the outside corners. Eventually one or both corners would begin to tear apart. This failure is like taking several sheets of typing paper in both hands and tearing them in half. Early signs of this failure were manifested by the popping of particles to form a narrow, inverted trough along the highly stressed outside corners of the multiple-entry system. Whenever this happened the outside entries were permanently abandoned and the mining system was reduced by two entries. Hence, a ten-entry mine became an eight-entry mine. Eventually the outside entries would begin to progressively tear or cut, sometimes for as far as two thousand feet or more. This deliberately induced failure could take many months to stress out, finally bringing an end to the "cutter."

When in active failure, a cutter can be like being in a war zone with an endless drumbeat of violent earth movement and endless noise. Surprisingly enough this tearing can be desirable, since stress is shifted from a complex and sometimes difficult-to-manage configuration involving mixed components of both tension and compression, to one involving only the singular component of compression. In practical terms, the entire overburdened load is largely placed directly onto the strong pillars. Given favorable floor, roof and pillar conditions, this can result in more manageable strata control. The entire sequence involves the always-delicate art of managing mine roof failure.

I entered into this picture from my long-held position as fuels consultant for General Public Utilities Service Corporation. GPU had an indirect financial interest in mines that supplied their coal, and the miners at one mine were fearful of a then-active cutter located in outside entries parallel and adjacent to the entries that they were mining. Out of respect for the miners' wishes, management placed them in another section of the mine. The superintendent of the mine asked me to come in and look the situation over to see if I had any suggestions. Together we entered the temporarily abandoned section to observe the conditions. No sooner were we in a location to make some observations than all hell broke loose. We looked at each other and began a foot race toward the center entries and straight out of the section. We were probably at no time in danger, but the overpowering shaking, vibration and noise were unlike any cutters that I have seen before or since. Moreover, unlike being involved in an incoming military bombardment, modern coal miners frequently have no protective counterpart equivalent to the soldier's foxhole. Since there is no hole to jump into, the coal miner must depend on his athleticism, speed and nimbleness to reach safety.

The Lexington Cemetery in Lexington, Kentucky, is a cemetery that time will not forget. The magnificent flowering trees and shrubs explode each year on the Fourth of July prompting an annually scheduled drive-through. Many bring lunches. Thousands of people cram the front gates to view the spectacle from their slow-moving cars, and some are turned away. It's like nothing Jo and I have ever seen before.

During our first visit to the annual drive-through, I spotted an old familiar statue high on a pedestal. It was that of Henry Clay, an exact match for the one on Sharp Mountain towering over the south side of Pottsville. Henry Clay was a lifetime Lexington resident and arguably this nation's greatest early-nineteenth-century statesman. Clay's statue belonged at his gravesite in Lexington, but what was a replica of his statue doing in Pottsville?

Recently, Pottsville raised money and completely refurbished their 160-year-old masterpiece. Among many similar statues, Clay's statues in Pottsville and Lexington are the only two still known to be in existence. Like the Yuengling Brewery, America's oldest brewery, and the John O'Hara Home, Henry Clay's statue is a Pottsville landmark.

From visits to Henry Clay's mansion in Lexington and his other shrines, I learned that Clay was responsible for passing legislation that placed tariffs on certain imported goods. For America's then-struggling heavy industry—coal, iron, timber, etc.—this legislation spelled prosperity. Foreign nations were now being asked to send money by investing in the bond offerings of American companies rather than products. It was a new ball game. Few stood to prosper more than the Anthracite Region of Pennsylvania, and folks living in Pottsville during the 1830s and 1840s were especially grateful. Using borrowed money from Britain and Europe, the young America could now build the railroads and other infrastructure needed to connect our large East Coast markets to our abundant inland coal, timber and iron ore resources. We were no longer a costal nation!

For a profile in courage, patriotism and tragedy, a study of the life of this great man and his deeply religious wife Lucretia is strongly recommended. Although there are many prominent Clays in Kentucky, Henry Clay has no direct descendants. His senior son died fighting in the battle of Buena Vista in the Mexican War. Another son was in and out of mental institutions. His favorite daughter died during childbirth. This incident drove him into deep depression. Friends along the New Jersey seacoast took him in for several months to help him regain his sanity. He and Lucretia were always precariously close to bankruptcy and the loss of Ashland, their still-beautiful estate in Lexington. He ran for president of the United States four times, never won, and on one occasion missed being elected by only a few votes. Clay owned slaves, like most landowners of that time, but unlike many of his contemporaries his will provided for their freedom.

To me, Henry Clay is the father of this nation's coal industry and, in the broader sense, all of this nation's heavy industry. He was one of a kind.

Who could ever forget the reports of early mining activities under the cities of Scranton and Wilkes-Barre in the northern Anthracite Region of Pennsylvania? Coal measures in the northern district were relatively flat compared to those of the highly faulted and pitched Pottsville area. Much costly dead work was needed to get into a vein, but once the vein was penetrated, mining became more predictable. These flat mining conditions frequently permitted the adoption of mining methods employed in the well-established bituminous coal mining industry. By contrast, the Pottsville area required very little costly dead work because the many miles of coal outcrops permitted relatively easy penetration into the vein, but as mining progressed it became more costly and less predictable.

As a boy I used to go into the basement of my great aunt and uncle's home on Electric Avenue in Scranton, and listen to the drills operating in the mines. For me, but not for the locals, this was an awesome and eerie experience. It was all so close, and yet so far away. My great uncle Nick Klein was the chief engineering draftsman for the D.L. and H. Railroad, and one of my early role models. While searching for references for a research paper in the University of Kentucky Library in the late 1990s, I stumbled upon some of the very first reports of the no-longer-existent United States Bureau of Mines. The reports chronicled the results of more than one hundred years of mining under the northern district, prior to 1910. Suddenly, my first clear picture of the events underneath Scranton that produced the noise in the basement of Nick and Annie Klein's home more than fifty years earlier came into focus. I was hooked, and quickly forgot the original reason for my being in the library, and read on and on. These revelations were captivating.

The expanding anthracite coal market created a demand that caused people to take their limited resources, gain control over any available adjacent properties, and sink a vertical shaft down to the first coal seam. Thirteen shafts were at one time located within the small confines of the city of Scranton. When the mine operator ran out of coal in the first seam, which was all too rapid because of the small acreage, he would simply sink the shaft deeper and penetrate into the second seam. In some places this search for coal reached great depths, penetrating as many as thirteen seams. When no more seams could be found, the operators would load railroad cars with rock after discharging their cargo of coal at distant markets, and return the rock to the mine. The rock was then lowered underground and used to construct stone walls around the remaining coal pillars. When construction of the walls was complete, the coal was removed from within the walls and shipped out for sale. This left the entire support system for holding up the population centers dependent upon the undependable man-made underground stonework. No wonder they called Wilkes-Barre the "city on stilts."

Graphic pictures in the early reports of the Bureau of Mines showed hospitals and schools with big cracks and tilted on lopsided angles. Of course, they were condemned. This was indeed the ultimate example of greed, where the inability of people to focus on a coordinated plan caused both starvation mining and an environmental disaster. I suppose a few people got rich. One good thing that came out of this saga was the Scranton Engineer's Club, which preceded the American Institute of Mining, Metallurgical and Petroleum Engineers. The mining experiences underneath the northern district and other mining areas were carefully observed and reported in early mining engineering technical publications sponsored by these societies. These early reports frequently served as a foundation for greatly improving our ability to mine minerals in a manner that would be of the greatest possible benefit to mankind.

Who could forget those frisky first-line mine foremen, both in and outside of the mine, who were almost always totally aerobic?

Because their jobs required them to be in many places during the course of a shift, and mobile transportation was not always available, foremen relied on their legs and lungs. Deep mine foremen could maintain a fast-paced walk, erect or stooped-over, for miles. Surface plant foremen could run up and down steps for almost endless periods. Mine management found a certain unspoken glee in pairing their best mine athletes with trips of visiting "city slickers and green horns." Events leading into these setups were always easily detectable to the more experienced mine traveler. One mine foreman/athlete would lead the trip setting a fast pace, while a second would bring up the rear, urging on the increasingly lengthening line of hapless stragglers. The moans and groans coming from the fellow travelers were taken as a measure of manhood, according to some standards. A fellow traveler who stayed with the lead foreman was quietly seen as a real man. Excuses for poor performance could be catalogued as follows: I'm getting old; I need to quit smoking; I gotta loose some weight; I didn't know I was in such poor condition; I should not have drunk so much last night, etc. The mine insiders found these visits worthy subjects for future discussion and comparative evaluation.

Few can forget the sometimes closely confined space of coal mining, and the body contortions and mental focus needed to achieve mobility. In coal mining you stand up, bend over or crawl, depending on the height of the mine and the equipment used. Seven-foot-high mines are totally walkable in the normally erect position, three-and-a-half- to six-foot-high mines require that the miner shuffle in increasingly bent-over positions, while mines with less than three and a half feet of mining height will force the miner to bend far over, approaching his physical limit, or begrudgingly retreat to crawling on hands and knee pads.

The body was not made for prolonged periods of fast-paced, non-erect mobility, and there is always an impulse to stand up straight and reclaim our primordial upright position. In doing so, even the very best mine yogis and contortionists frequently bump their helmet-encased heads against mine roof bolts and timbers, a jolting experience when traveling at fast pace. Indeed, I am grateful for the many striations that are on my helmet and not on my head, and one must wonder what it must have been like when our miner forebears were still using canvas caps.

The closely encumbered space of coal mining frequently requires much mental control. Perhaps the best advice is to think small. I remember visiting a deep mine in England, where the mine manager told me a story involving Britain's Royal Marines. Apparently the Royal Marines were regularly run through some of the deepest and most confining sections of his mine as an exercise to help them develop their mental and physical endurance. If needed, temporary marginal ventilation and hot working conditions could also be readily arranged to enhance the exercise and more closely approach human panic levels. I did not doubt for a moment that my farsighted and patriotic hosts might have overlooked this possibility.

To my surprise, this tough old mining hand expressed concern about the condition of the very best soldiers. He found that some of the biggest and strongest marines had to be helped from the mine. We both agreed that this might be the ultimate test of soldiering, and the marines will be much better people as a result of the experience.

※

As always, there were those eccentric characters in our ever-changing coal mining industry. Otto, who reportedly was seventy-seven years old and lived in a shack, worked every day of his life and at the time was cleaning mine track. The shack was of his own construction at the local dump. Otto showered free of cost in the mine washhouse, ate food that selected hotels delivered to the dump, and seldom talked. He could still outwork anyone when cleaning mine track over an eight-hour shift, was reported to be worth millions, and nobody knew where he kept his money. Some thought he sent it to relatives in Austria, while others thought that he kept it in cans at the dump. Otto obtained his mismatched and odorous clothing from the dump, and his only known expenditure was for tobacco. When I could get Otto to talk I found him to be a deeply reflective and almost spiritual person.

Another character, known as "Dirty Mouth," reportedly dropped his false teeth in the mine ditch after relieving himself, fished his teeth out of the ditch, wiped them off on his filthy mine jacket and put them back into his mouth. Dirty Mouth also had a permanent pouch in the side of his mouth, developed from years of chewing oversize wads of tobacco. He was known to recharge his wad by sticking his finger into his mouth and throwing the spent cud several yards with his index finger. The fresh charge would be pressed firmly into place with the same finger. He was reported to be able to eat his lunch while chewing tobacco. Dirty Mouth never married.

Cowboy, an incredibly hard-working Illinois welder, lived in two trailers with his wife and many children from several marriages, rebuilt wrecked automobiles scattered all over his one-acre lot, quoted the Bible, swore off booze and women years earlier, and respected his wife but always referred to her as "the old lady." He always wore a cowboy hat, boots, belt, shirt and overalls to both church and work. Cowboy, because of his many responsibilities, frequently came on shift late, much to the irritation of management. When he finally arrived, he worked like a demon. Cowboy set records for welding productivity, much to the irritation of the other welders. With both management and co-workers angry, Cowboy agreed to work the early morning hours, out of sight of all, where his performance would be based on productivity and not time on the job. Always the clown, he earned begrudging respect from all of his associates. After all, who would not be impressed with his efforts to single-handedly change his life, and the life of his family, for the better? God was on his side.

Ben was the general superintendent of mines. He laughed loud and often at both good news and bad news throughout each long and crisis-filled day. Through no fault of his own, Ben was managing mining operations where the coal was very soft and contained excessive fines. Although problems with fines are present to some extent with all coal mining, his were excessive. High fines content adds billions of more particles to the product. The immediate result of this cussed geology was more dust, handling difficulties, flow blockages, excess moisture and high-cost coal cleaning. Company efforts to reduce these costly problems involved much on-site experimentation, all of which interfered with management. No quitter, Ben was trying to do it all while recovering from several heart attacks, probably brought on by overwork. Apparently exhausted from making too many weighty decisions, and after a fifty-year career of working in the industry, Ben decided to go out laughing.

Walt was hired to manage the tires of the company's truck fleet. After only a few minutes of conversation, Walt quickly revealed himself as an oily, pompous and gross misfit. Walt soon turned the rugged mine roads into speedways and used his personal automobiles to set an example of how to drive at high speed while swerving in and out of the giant revved-up trucks. Most staffers and union men found the elevated speed levels more than they were prepared to cope with. After a company dignitary and chief stockholder nearly got flattened by a truck during a visit, things began to change. A mandated review showed that although paid a generous allowance for mileage, Walt quietly billed the company for numerous unauthorized sets of new super-quality tires for his family cars, claiming that his responsibilities demanded additional expense money. After a front office interview the word was soon out that Walt and the company had reached an amicable agreement concerning Walt's outplacement.

Old Shank, at seventy-six years old, was considered to be the brilliant mechanical engineer who, it was claimed, was personally responsible for designing every successful process and machine in the company. Unsuccessful processes were apparently designed by other people, no longer with the company. Old Shank had clearly attained a level approaching deification. Old Shank, who always wore a bow tie and arm bands, was first to arrive at work each day and last to leave the engineering office in the evening. He spoke very little and seldom socialized. Folks claimed that he worked for the company from the day it was founded. Even the old timers did not seem to know whom he reported to or what he was doing. Some claimed that he was a spy for the president. What made Old Shank worthy of mention was his once- or twice-a-week habit of looking up from his drafting board and bursting out into hysterical and overpowering laughter mixed with tears. The hysteria would last about two minutes before Old Shank would once again lapse back into his patented detached silence. This condition was a source of endless discussion and almost unlimited speculation among the staffers. Some were certain that he was losing his mind, while others claimed that it was an unfailing mark of genius.

Leo, the seventy-six-year-old mine superintendent, occasionally went on a solo tour of his sprawling facility. Whenever Leo stopped for a close look at anything, rumors quickly circulated that the people responsible for the item under review would be fired. This had a powerful short-term effect on mine productivity. It was apparent that Leo was still useful to the company. Leo seldom initiated conversation, and when he did it was strictly work related. I once attempted to wish Leo success prior to one of his famous inspections, only to be subjected to a long, blank stare. When nothing came back, I was absolutely sure that with Leo "children were to be seen and not heard." Leo was an old timer who apprenticed for long periods of time at every conceivable level of company engineering, beginning as a back sight rod man on an underground surveying crew. Leo probably viewed people like me as "upstarts." Surprisingly enough, employees at the mine had a towering respect for him. One bright and sunny day, Leo grabbed me by the arm, pulled me in close and told me that I was doing a great job. A few days earlier I had implemented a quick fix and permanent solution to a major coal production problem that periodically idled both his mine and preparation plants. Now I knew the secret of his long and untarnished tenure, he was probably smarter than the rest of us.

The best union jobs at most mines are those of the pump man and lamp man. These jobs come with the highest seniority, are frequently filled long before the mine ever produces a single ton of coal, last for the life of the mine, and come with a full five-day work week with much overtime. Jobholders are frequently relatives of key mine officials, or relatives of former landowners who yielded control of their mining rights in exchange for money and job security. These are the ultimate insider positions. Tired and deserving old coal miners were barred from these jobs because of hearing loss caused by years of underground drilling and blasting.

Chuck was the clean-cut kid who married the wealthy daughter of a high company official. Chuck made many reckless and impulsive spot decisions that cost the company a small fortune. Repeated efforts to have him removed seemed to run out of steam immediately above the first level of management. Efforts were further complicated since Chuck was always the first to publicly admit his mistakes, never lied, cussed or lost his temper, and was active in his church. What kind of a coal-pushing bully would want to fire such a nice, popular and well-liked husband and father? Word was always pushed back through the first level of management that Chuck was a very bright young man who was entitled to make a few youthful mistakes, and who was viewed at the highest possible levels as having considerable long-term potential for the future of the company. Years later Chuck worked his way into several boardrooms, where he became known as a corporate cost cutter.

The "Goat Woman" raised goats and was widely known for stealing company coal from loaded railroad cars stored on tracks located behind her home. The Goat Woman, equipped with a large wheelbarrow and shovel, would mount railroad cars, at considerable risk, after dark and scoop coal off the cars into the wheelbarrow located about twenty feet below. Evidence of her larceny became apparent the next day when officials were forced to clean up the track spillage that developed from her sloppy, high-altitude wheelbarrow loading. Officials who approached her company home were met by dogs, an endless stream of profanities and threats to get her "old man," a powerful giant of a man and contract miner, to come out and beat them up. Reports soon circulated that the company was unable to find anyone willing to serve the Goat Woman with further legal notices, bringing an end to the threat to her long-term supply of free coal.

seeing the future of the
anthracite industry

4

In the late fall of 1948, during my senior year of high school, Mr. Edward G. Fox, who was the president of the influential Philadelphia and Reading Coal and Iron Company (P&RC&I) talked to our class during an assembly period. His talk would determine the direction of my life. This visionary presided over a mining company that was spun off of the parent Reading Company in1921, when the government declared the Reading Company a monopoly. The Reading Company was broken up into the P&RC&I Company, the mining unit, and the Reading Railroad, the railroad unit. The government claimed that the Reading Company, and others like it, deliberately operated their mines at a loss, in order to eliminate competition from non-railroad-affiliated coal mines, while making up for any losses by charging excessively for the haulage of coal on their railroads.

In the 1870s the Reading Company was the richest company on earth. When Mr. Fox spoke to my class, the spun-off P&RC&I Company, though powerful, was facing numerous problems. These were clearly foreseeable by Mr. Fox, but not by the general public. Problems included the greatly increased availability of more costly but convenient oil and gas. Other problems were the aging anthracite industry, now over 120 years old, and an aging workforce in an industry perceived by many as dirty and dangerous. Mr. Fox knew that the future of the industry depended on holding on to or minimizing market share losses to oil and gas. Effort was to be directed at rallying the coal industry into developing and marketing better, more automated combustion equipment. Unfortunately, most initial installations of this fine equipment would invariably cost more than the lower-cost hand-fired coal heating systems and totally automated oil and gas heating systems, which the new anthracite combustion equipment was intended to replace.

To offset this problem, the cost of delivered anthracite coal would have to be reduced. Mr. Fox knew that most of the surface and deep mining industry had to be renewed. This was to be done by expanding surface mining and replacing old deep mines with fewer and more productive mines. Both surface and deep mines would employ the most modern technology in the best reserves. Moreover, Mr. Fox knew that the large and aging company management and workforce would soon retire and that new blood was needed. His 1948 visit to Pottsville High School was part of his plan to implement this goal.

Mr. Fox's talk was upbeat. He was looking for quality students capable of successfully completing a degree in a nationally ranked coal mining engineering department, such as the one offered at Penn State. He said that students who qualified would be provided support through a pioneering work-study plan. Suddenly, Nanna's many stories about Phil Bettinger and the Phoenix Park Mine, mother's stories about geology and my own long-held notion that a degree in mining engineering might provide a means to build a hometown career, all came together. This was an offer that I had to pursue. Dad strongly opposed my decision, since he remembered the way that his dad lived and died in what he believed was a terrible industry. Nevertheless, after my reassurances that things were not the same as they once were, he said that he would support my decision.

I took a series of tests and interviews with P&RC&I Company executives and awaited the outcome. The results were positive, and

I was told to report to the employment office to begin a series of summer jobs. These work-training jobs continued for four years up until the time of my graduation. I never learned so much in such a short period of time. Rotated through numerous surveying jobs, preparation plant jobs and mining jobs, I worked at and observed more that twenty key elements of mining.

Some of these diverse jobs included performing regular maintenance of surface and deep mining equipment, operating underground drills, laying railroad track, cleaning ditches, timbering, rock bolting, mucking rock, hauling supplies, observing blasting, following the fire boss during inspections, accompanying the processing plant superintendent, accompanying the divisional superintendents of both the Pottsville and Mahoney City divisions, surveying above and below ground, working in the main engineering office, trouble-shooting at the coal processing plant and assisting the coal laboratory. In addition to this excellent training, the wages that the company paid me provided for all of my expenses at Penn State. During this period, I qualified for mining papers and joined the United Mine Workers of America.

On graduation from Penn State, and despite other better-paying job offers, I decided to take a position as assistant to the divisional superintendent of the Pottsville district where I served under Mr. Dallas E. Ingersoll. After four years at Penn State, punctuated by frequent weekend and summer visits home, my young wife Jo and I realized we needed a full-time presence in Pottsville, to be near to dad, Nanna and my sister Liz. I was Mr. Ingersoll's "leg" man, a position that gave me great engineering and management exposure, and allowed me to continue to grow in stature as an engineer in mine management. I had the opportunity to work with some of the very best mine and processing plant superintendents in what I now believe, in hindsight, was the most diverse and complex mining industry in the world.

Jo and I settled in an apartment house on Mahantongo Street in Pottsville. We were located not far from my grandmother Bettinger's home on Grant Street, where I was raised, and where she lived with my dad, his new wife and my sister Liz. Down the street from our apartment was Mr. Fox's stately home, our historic family church of Saint John the Baptist, the home of John O'Hara, the great novelist of the 1920s and 1930s and the landmark Yuengling Brewery. Our neighborhood was stately, though dated, and a place of much history. It was a good place to be.

By 1955 it was becoming increasingly apparent that the industry was steadily losing market share to oil and gas, despite a massive regional effort to save it. Shorter work time for miners, sometimes as little as one day a week, and the permanent closure of the higher-cost mines were two ominous signs. When the historic Lytle Mine could no longer afford to pump the ever-increasing volumes of water infiltrating through extensive old workings located at higher elevations, the citizens raised $200,000 for the purchase of powerful stage pumps.

The Lytle Mine, measured vertically from the shaft collar, was the deepest coal mine in the region, and possibly North America's all-time deepest coal mine. The Lytle was not only handling its own water, but it was also handling the water from a large number of other operating deep mines located at higher elevations. If this mine were to close, other mines would soon be flooded with water, causing a chain-reaction collapse of this important coal-producing district. In addition, many deep wells were sunk and pumps were installed in the wells throughout much of the coal region. Huge volumes of water were pumped from these wells and discharged into hundreds of miles of flumes in a late and desperate effort to remove the water and transport it, once and for all, out of the region. Prior to this time water was pumped out of one mine only to have it infiltrate the connecting, surrounding mines in a senseless recycling of water that greatly added to the cost of pumping.

To find new ways to mine and use coal, the United States Bureau of Mines established a research laboratory at Schuylkill Haven, Pennsylvania. Again, these late and desperate efforts undoubtedly reduced mining costs in some areas and slowed down the decline of the industry, but the erosion of coal markets was unrelenting. Long-established coal dealers began selling bulk oil, and utilities began selling pipeline gas. Coal furnace builders diversified into the construction of oil and gas furnaces. Pipeline gas was now replacing the long-used local gas made from anthracite coal. Although anthracite is a very clean burning fuel, second only to gas, it left ashes, which were not always easily disposed. Clearly, the handwriting was on the wall. It was time for Jo and me to begin to think about our future. Leaving family behind in Pottsville, where mother died in 1945, where our daughter Beth was born, and where my forebears lived and called home for over 110 years was not an easy decision for us to make.

Pottsville was one of the very best locations for a mining engineer, with a cultural environment far ahead of most mining camps, and with mining complexities that challenged the innovation capabilities of the very best mining engineers. I also had to give up my long-held personal goal, which was to become president, like Mr. Fox, of a major anthracite coal-mining company. It was clear that an almost endless round of layoffs, mine closures, downsizing, bankruptcies and reorganizations lay ahead. Engineers are builders, and during downsizings we merely maintain. The new environment clearly offered more opportunities for legal advice, accounting and politicians.

I accepted a job with the United Electric Coal Companies at Canton, Illinois. A few years later we returned to Penn State, where I completed graduate school and went to work for the United States Steel Company Applied Research Laboratory at Monroeville, Pennsylvania. In 1961 I began a long career in academics at West Virginia University and the University of Kentucky.

This great mining region was about to go into a long decline, and it would not recover within the memory of any living residents, or their children. Someday, perhaps hundreds of years from now during a future fuel or carbon shortage crisis, this huge reserve of coal, which lies at considerable depths and underwater, will be mined. Billions of tons of anthracite coal are left unmined in the Pennsylvania Anthracite Region, with more than half located in the deep and steeply folded southern region surrounding Pottsville. Future planners will need to prepare to re-mine the region long ahead of any fuel crisis, since this project will be enormous, and will not respond to a quick fix solution. Mother Nature does not give up her mineral wealth easily.

As in many other parts of the world, society will not leave this energy treasure trove idle. I speculate that the cities and cemeteries will be moved to entirely new locations, and giant surface excavating machines, together with some advanced deep mining systems, will recover the remaining coal. This new age of mining will last for more than one hundred years. These excavations will be carefully designed, and will serve as gigantic storage areas for an endless supply of future high-quality water. Unlike in the past, the new extractive industry will offer only a small number of underground jobs. The many new mining jobs will be in clean work and will be widely spread through the engineering, construction and sale of mining, safety and environmental equipment and through land, water and fuel management.

After driving Nanna hundreds of miles on Sunday afternoon sightseeing tours in the late 1940s and early1950s, including repeated attempts to drive to her old home in Phoenix Park, when I returned in the 1990s, I found that all the old familiar routes were barricaded by gates. The posted gates indicated the property limits of active mining sites. The old walking trails were now overgrown and thoroughly vegetated. We assumed that Phoenix Park was a no-longer-existent mining patch, perhaps replaced by surface mining; but the images of Nanna's long ago laptop stories never completely faded from memory.

One night while sitting in the Pottsville Club with Jo and Major Robert and Betty Shuman, we talked about anthracite mining history. I mentioned that grandfather Phil Bettinger III was a mine boss at the Phoenix Park Mine in the early 1900s. Bob said that their son Dan recently lived there, and that Phoenix Park was alive and well. With Bob, Dan, his wife Brenda and son, we took a Sunday morning tour of this storied mining patch. We reached our goal through an unmarked road that was completely unfamiliar. Everything fell into place. Nanna's home on bosses' row was still there and in fine condition. Located on top of a hill overlooking the village at the end of a winding, dead-end street, it was just as Nanna portrayed it to me in her bedtime stories nearly seventy years earlier. The view down onto the village from her yard on bosses' row was, for me, a very spiritual and moving experience. For a moment, she was once again there with me. The old shaft head frame, no longer spinning, has been replaced with a protective grate covering the still firmly in place mine shaft collar. A rock dropped down the shaft hit water in about a second, indicating that the long-idle mine was now serving as a potential and vast storage area for future water supplies.

Phoenix Park, now resurrected from the shadows of my mind, is not on any road maps and there are no route markers showing the way. This is the reason why a piece of living history has been hidden and preserved for more than a century. It is the reason why some well-traveled person living just six miles away might not know of its existence. It is the reason why people want to live there in their modest but well-kept homes, coupled with the village fire department, social center, church, playground and open areas. This patch that time forgot offers residents a place to hide from change while enjoying the offerings and rewards of the real world located just a few miles away. The folks at Phoenix Park want it that way. This is a place that some folks in the real world would not understand.

It is my hope and desire that the readers of this book will be enriched with a deepened knowledge of our coal-mining industry, what it means to our nation and its people and how it has contributed almost infinitely to the quality of our lives. Always remember that if we don't grow it, or mine it, we don't have it. I also hope that the reader will not forget the great sacrifices made by our coal miners and their families in giving birth to the American Industrial Revolution.

mining in images

The Ellangowan Mine Hoisting Slope in 1915. This is typical of the lifting devices used at that time. *Schuylkill County Historical Society*

Removal of a body from the St. Clair Colliery in 1934. Note the improved helmets of varied designs and the modern helmet lights. The two helmets on the left were designed to permit ventilation during heavy physical work. These were preferred by the coal miners. The helmet on the right was frequently worn by supervisors. *Schuylkill County Historical Society.*

Early coal-loading machine. Because bituminous coal in the United States is generally flat laying with favorable stratigraphic conditions, automated mining became possible. Today, our deep bituminous mines are more like coal factories than coal mines. In fact, they are safer to work in than most conventional factories. Frequently these machines mine coal much faster that it can be carried away. Our deep bituminous coal mines produce about twenty-eight tons of coal per man day versus two to three tons of coal per man day during the very best years of anthracite mining. The author spent much of his career consulting in the international bituminous coal industry. The following photos show some of the extensive array of equipment available to rapidly mine bituminous coal. *Joy Mining Manufacturing.*

First Shuttle Car. This underground truck hauls coal from the mining face to the out-by loading point. Most shuttle cars are attached to a sometimes cumbersome, battery-powered electric cable. With regulatory permission, diesel powered shuttle cars are now available. *Joy Mining Manufacturing.*

Continuous Miner. This photo shows a continuous miner with cutting head ready to chew out coal. *Joy Mining Manufacturing.*

Joy Mining Manufacturing.

Giant Continuous Miner. *Joy Mining Manufacturing.*

Long Wall Mining Machinery. If ever there was a doubt about whether bituminous coal mining was an underground factory, this is the system that removed all doubts. This collection of machinery consists of a mobile cutting device, shields to thoroughly protect the men and an armored conveyor to carry the coal away from the face. The entire system might be thirty-yards wide by six-hundred- yards long. It slices away the coal face broad side in slabs of two to four feet or more. The armored conveyor strains to carry the coal away. This glutton produces tons per man day ranging well into the hundreds. Costs of the system may amount to thirty million dollars for a six-hundred-yard unit. This system relegates the well-known surface mining productivity to the bush leagues. The seam is prepared by using long drill holes in advance of mining and forcing water under pressure into the holes to purge gas and dust from the seam. A great volume of air is blown across the face to insure the complete removal of gas and dust from the workings. The real danger here is getting a cold. This is one of the big reasons why the deep bituminous coal mining industry offers a working environment second to none. *Joy Mining Manufacturing.*

Long Wall System. Another view of the system. *Joy Mining Manufacturing.*

epilogue

On February 6, 1986, I came home at noon, an unusual action, in order to pick up some overlooked papers needed for a university function scheduled for that afternoon. Jo was in town keeping some previously scheduled appointments. As I was about to leave to go back to work, my son Joe's wife Barb called. She was very distraught. Barb said that a terrible report was coming over Pittsburgh television about five men being killed in a mine disaster at Consol's Loveridge Mine near Mannington, West Virginia, and that Joe's name was mentioned. What an ugly way to learn about a possible tragedy. I told Barb that there had to be a mistake, and that I would call Consol to find the truth. The truth was slow coming, but it did come.

Yes, five engineers, including Joe, were presumed dead during a site visit to obtain information for the preparation of an engineering estimate to repair a stockpile-loading boom. I was told that the coal stockpile that they were standing on collapsed and that all five were buried and presumed dead. I was sickened. What will I tell Jo when she comes home? I called Barb and we both went into depression. I waited and waited. In what seemed like forever, Jo finally came through the garage door. I grabbed her, hugged her and whispered the news repeatedly in her ear. We both

Joseph W. Leonard IV, the author's son. This picture was taken during his attendance as a cadet at Linsley Military Institute, Wheeling, WV. Joe graduated from Linsley and later received his B.S. and M.S. degrees in mining engineering from West Virginia University, Morgantown, WV. At the time of his death he was assistant preparation engineer for Consolidation Coal Company's Northern West Virginia Division.

fell to the floor and sobbed. There was no comfort. We waited for a miracle, but no miracles were forthcoming. Many hours after the disaster all five bodies were recovered; the coroner ruled that they died in an air pocket of suffocation. At age twenty-nine, Joe was the youngest in the group to die; he left Barbara, age twenty-seven, Mary Jo, age four and Joe V, age two.

On the snowy evening of February 6, 1986, Dr. Dave Newman, a new member of our mining faculty and a friend, drove Jo and me to Morgantown in our car while we sat in the back seat, held hands, embraced and wept. We worked with Barb, family and friends to complete all arrangements. With five mining people dead, the Morgantown area was a site of much grief. Joe was buried from Saint Mary's Church at Star City, West Virginia. Life for Jo, Barb, Mary Jo, Joe V and me would never be the same. Life for all of the loving members of our family would never be the same. The loss was sudden and completely unexpected. Joe had a job that appeared to be free of any hazardous situations, so much so that I no longer worried about his safety. The most enduring part of this tragedy was that Mary Jo and Joey would never come to know the warm, decent and loving father that they lost, a father who just loved to "tote" his kids around, on one or both arms, even when doing his household chores.

We took a lease on an apartment in Morgantown with a swimming pool, so that we could be there and be available to support Barb and the kids. Jo gave much time to this project while I took all the leave time allowed to me by the university. In this regard the university bent all the rules, and was more than generous. We considered giving up my job and going back to Morgantown. I no longer cared about chairing the department. The severe shock of losing a son in mining, while giving entirely too much of life's quality time to help bring about the birth of a mining department, was more than anyone should be required to give. The administrative nightmare that we managed to overcome now seemed to be just another wasted exercise.

I asked myself why anyone, with our very sad family mining history, would permit his son to go into mining. The answer always comes back that mining at the time of Joe's entry into the industry was rapidly becoming the safest industrial work environment in the United States; and, at the time of his death, was nearly unsurpassed for safety. The answer always comes back that only when Joe was well established in mining did I learn from very old, distant family members and old mine and church records about the tragic deaths of our sixteen-year-old grand-uncle John and our forty-four-year-old great-great grandfather Phillip. Unless one believes in predestination, the answer always comes back that no one can read the future, for if we could, each of us would dodge unpleasantries and subsequently introduce humankind into a form of weakness and endless decline that is not part of God's plan.

Our new and more settled life as a faculty member and professor of mining engineering was later rewarded with election to the first mining engineering foundation distinguished professorship. I held this position as the first mining engineering foundation distinguished professor emeritus until my retirement from the University of Kentucky on December 31, 1998. During and after my term as chairman, many new professional awards were forthcoming, and our home-office wall is covered with these citations, but things can never again be the same.

The nature of mining engineering involves the management of rock, and as such is the engineering branch of the science that we know as geology. Our future mining engineers will be as diverse and broadly educated as ever, but they will be even more broadly educated "rock or particle" engineers. After all, this is what mining engineering is all about. There is a fundamental reason why other engineers humorously refer to mining engineers as the liberal artists of the engineering college. We deal with the engineering and science of particles, and particles are like people in that no two have ever been created alike. We explore, break, stabilize, transport and separate particles in an environmentally and economically acceptable manner. Management of particles is even more fundamentally random than the management of people, and this background tends to "gene program" mining engineers for future management, especially management involving the mixing of people and technology.

Moreover, of all the engineering disciplines, mining engineers have the least control over our design. Our design is not man-made like circuit boards and bridges, but is hidden by Mother Nature under an invisible mantle of dirt and rock, where all too frequently surprises await. We can explore this hidden world, but the realities of economics insure that knowledge can never be complete. As a mining engineer I have much empathy for the physician, who also has problems seeing through a frequently hidden design organized by a much higher authority. The great hope for mining engineers and physicians is that instrumentation that allows us to "see through" and "feel" our opaque operating environment is getting better.

To date our many wonderful friends have contributed over $70,000 to the Joseph W. Leonard IV Memorial Scholarship located in the West Virginia University Loyalty Permanent Endowment Fund. Joe's scholarship will provide seven $1,000-per-year grants to mining students in perpetuity. Readers wishing to contribute to the scholarship fund may contact the Mining Engineering Department at West Virginia University by calling 304-293-5695. Contributions of as little as $10 in 1950 are listed each year in the annual Loyalty Permanent Endowment Funds updated listings and sent out to hundreds of people and organizations. Hence, this unique fund memorializes contributors in perpetuity. Joe is permanently remembered with a memorial plaque, located on the wall of the new College of Mineral and Energy Resources building at West Virginia University. I dedicated my final book, *Coal Preparation V*, which was known as the "bible of the coal industry," to Joe IV and the four other engineers who died at Loveridge.

The 170-year journey of the Leonard family through the history of American coal mining was over.

about the author

Joe Leonard III is a fifth-generation coal miner and mining engineering foundation distinguished professor emeritus of the University of Kentucky. After graduation from Penn State, he worked in both the American anthracite and bituminous coal mining industries. He advanced from mine laborer to assistant to the divisional superintendent of mines in the Pennsylvania anthracite industry and later to assistant coal processing engineer in the Illinois bituminous industry. After returning to and completing graduate work at Penn State, Joe worked as a research engineer in coal and coke for United States Steel's Applied Research Laboratory, prior to entering into a long academic career serving as dean, director, chairman, distinguished professor and professor at West Virginia University and the University of Kentucky.

Joe has numerous books, reports, publications, patents, awards, citations and certifications. Among his books are *Coal Preparation, Volumes III, IV* and *V*, which were published in 1968, 1979 and 1991. These books are collectively known as the "bible of the coal industry," with tens of thousands located on bookshelves all over the world. He is also a long-term author of the "Coal" section of *World Book Encyclopedia*. A consultant and visitor to more than three hundred mines in sixteen countries around the world, Joe Leonard III served for twenty-seven years as secretary-treasurer of the Society of Mining Engineers Central Appalachian Section, one of the nation's largest coal mining regions.

www.ingramcontent.com/pod-product-compliance
Lightning Source LLC
Chambersburg PA
CBHW060754100426

42813CB00004B/819